The Less I Hold

Rosemerry Wahtola Trommer

Poems

with many blessings,

Rosemerry

TURKEY BUZZARD PRESS

Acknowledgments

My thanks to the editors of the following publications who originally accepted for publication some of the poems found in this book.

Bigger Than They Appear: Anthology of Very Short Poems, ed. Katerina Stoykova-Klemer, for "All in an Effort to Not Think About"; *Clover* for "Four Questions And" and "While from the Kitchen Wafts the Scent of Something Burning on the Stove"; *Cradle Songs: An Anthology of Poems on Motherhood*, eds. Sharmagne Leland-St. John and Rachelle Yousuf for "Because Sometimes I Get that No Gets Me Nowhere"; *Encore: Prize Poems of the NFSPS* for "Note to Self," "Even Accounting for Surface Friction," and "Before We Can Unlearn"; *Snakeskin* for "Instead of Dreaming"; *Heavy Bear* for "Just Because You Could Admit Something Once" and "Meanwhile in Another Garden"; *Letters from the World: Poems for Emily Dickinson*, ed. Jerome Charyn for "Postcard to Emily"; *The Nervous Breakdown* for "So I Keep on Reckoning"; *Pilgrimage* for "Ungraphable" (published as "Even Though I'm Partial to Words"); *Sugar Mule* for "At Four" and "Not That I Would Go Back."

I also extend my thanks to Kathryn and Joel Bass, Padma Thornlyre, Eric Trommer, and the Turkey Buzzards, who made this book possible. And I have so much appreciation for the communion of poets — O friends, I fling my arms open to you.

Cover Photo by Rosemerry Wahtola Trommer
Cover Design by Joel Bass
Author Photo by Kaycee Clark
Typesetting by Mad Blood
Printing by Rising Graphics, Evergreen, Colorado

The Less I Hold
by Rosemerry Wahtola Trommer
Published by Turkey Buzzard Press, Kittredge, Colorado
First Printing, 250 copies
Copyright © 2012 by Rosemerry Wahtola Trommer
ISBN 0-945884-41-9
Poetry

The Less I Hold

for my family

Foreword

"I know myself a spilling thing, a raveling . . . the vessel as it breaks," Rosemerry Wahtola Trommer writes in her poem, "Epistemology." These and many other lines from the passionate, attentive poems of *The Less I Hold* bring to mind Rainer Maria Rilke's "Ninth Elegy": ". . . because truly being here is so much; because everything here apparently needs us, this fleeting world, which in some strange way keeps calling to us. Us, the most fleeting of all." These evocative poems embody moments and hold up objects from the daily and tactile world until each yields radiance. The poet moves through her days in this sensuous world, helping us see and smell, taste and touch, listen—and sing.

Knowing, she discovers, is temporary, as wind reveals by "rearranging every / scrap I think I know." Longing, she sees, infiltrates fulfillment, which becomes longing again. Miracles, she finds, are canny creatures. They often appear when a sought thing is abandoned. And they come in the form of ripe apricots, a son's illness and "brightening voice," shoveling snow, a daughter's leaps into language—her first use of "-ing," with its ongoingness ("Mama chasing me"), and pears that refuse to be "tedious."

Astonishment, deep honesty, humility, unknowing, joy, and insight give Rosemerry Wahtola Trommer's voice its timbre. "I wanted oracles," she writes, and "in came tamarisk, rodents, dust." Rilke reminds us that "*Here* is the time for the *sayable.*" For "But. And. Everything." What can't be known or held is witnessed and luminous here.

Veronica Patterson
Thresh & Hold
Swan, What Shores?

Contents

Ashes We Are Not Yet

End Notes / 67

The Vessel as It Breaks

Acceptance

The whole time I shoveled the drive,
      snow was falling. Thick drapes of snow.
           Deepening snow. In every thin path I cleared,

new snow. I needed no higher teaching
      to understand things come and go.
           An endless process. And this was my place

in the world — transferring snow from one space
      to another, scraping out new emptinesses,
           watching them refill, stopping to stare

as the world grew new. Heaven coming down
      in great shovelfuls, more than one woman
           could possibly move. So humbling to see one's limit.

More humbling still to let it fade —
      not the limit itself,
           but the wanting to push it away.

Note to Self

Take the picture
from the desk
and put it
in the drawer.
It was true
to a moment
that was before,
but now as
lightning unzips
the sky and now
as the moon
is wholly new
you are no longer
the one the camera knew
with smile aslant
and lashes half-mast
in dreamy fringe.
It's okay to cry,
to want to grasp—
it's so human to want
to frame the past
and then attach it
to the fridge or set
it shrine-like on the shelf.
It is not so sad,
tell yourself,
to put the image away.
Notice how
much more you
look out the window.
Notice how much
more you look
at the vase.
And who is
doing the looking?
If sadness comes,
invite it for tea
and drink the dark

cup together. Take
turns sipping, take
your time. You'll
reach the bottom
soon enough.

Possibility

> *— time is a tree (this life one leaf)*
> *but love is the sky and i am for you*
> *just so long and long enough*
> *   –e.e. cummings, "[as freedom is a breakfast food]"*

At dinner, the boy says
in a matter of fact kind of way
Did you know that one day

the sun will burn out?
Yes, says the dad, and
the little girl starts to cry.

That means there will
be no more mornings,
she says. Oh sweetheart,

that's true, says the mom.
But it will not happen
for a long, long time,

long after you are gone.
This is no comfort
to the weeping one,

who, between bites
of cucumber and rice,
is tasting the loss of light,

the end of warmth,
this life only so long.
Outside, three leaves

fall, golden and full
of sun, but she does not
notice them.

Epistemology

I knew myself a swirl of ash
swept briskly by the wind—
like wings without the weight of birds,
like kites without their strings.

And I, who have been dead, tonight
I know myself the moon
with rings around it in the dark.
And I the darkness, too.

But I am also not the dark,
not moon, not ash, not kite,
not anything that can be held,
something beyond the night.

I know myself a spilling thing,
a raveling, a leak.
Call it blessing, call it luck
the vessel as it breaks.

Vivian Learns First Person Possessive

Two badminton rackets.
The orange one
she hands to me.

The red one
she holds in her fist
and says, *Mine.*

It's the first time
she says the word,
her introduction

to the language of want—
beyond naming the object
she shapes her desire

on her tongue and
claims the thing.
I gather my girl

into my arms and hold her
as if to say with touch what words
cannot. Mine. But. And. Everything

slips through our hands
eventually. There is no part
of speech to explain this,

no translation for the way that
things change. And they do.
Like a girl who just yesterday

belonged to the world. Like this woman
who loses what she once thought
she had, and watches the world

shift, one syllable at a time.

Because Sometimes I Get that No
Gets Me Nowhere

*You say yes to the sunlight and your pure fantasies, so you have to say
yes to the filth and the nausea. Everything is within you, gold and mud,
happiness and pain, the laughter of childhood and the apprehension of
death. Say yes to everything, shirk nothing, don't try to lie to yourself.*
— Hermann Hesse, translated by James Wright,
"Wandering"

It is not hard to say yes to the nausea
when it's your son's and he's lying on your belly
on the old wicker couch with foam cushions

and wave follows wave, and he shivers.
There is nothing romantic about this.
There is no way to say no. But there is love

and there is yes in the way that you carry him
to the shower, how he dangles his head
from the crook of your arms, how his legs

are more fabric than flesh. Do not squander this moment.
Cradle him as the warm water falls, choose to be naked
and covered in bile, to carry the weight of

the one that you love, to bathe his flushed face,
to be soft. To croon nothing but comfort. To baptize
yourself in this moment. Sun shaft in the window.

Gold in the spew. Yellow smell. Quiet splash on the wall.
Memorize the thin staffs of his ribs, the startling muscle
of his five-year-old limbs. Already you cannot explain

how you came this far, by some miracle to this small
white tub where the water heater has run out of warmth
and the boy loans all of his weight to your arms.

Postcard to Emily

How the old mountains drip with sunset.
— Emily Dickinson

Dear Emily,

It was just as you said, tonight,
the mountains rose and blue,
and in the shallow reservoir,
the herons dripping, too—
I did not mean to startle them
as grayly there they stood,
but on hushed feet I stepped myself
into their solitude.
Wing after wing they rowed away
into the muted dome
till all went dim—oh dark abyss!—
and we were held as one.

Blink

By accident she snipped
the amaryllis stalk

still crowned with buds
red and unopened. It happens.

It happens like this,
these moments in which

we do what we never
believed we would do

what were we thinking?
scissors in one hand,

and all that is newly undone
in the other.

Looking Back

When I think
of all that had to happen
to constellate this moment

in which I stand
beside the road
to cut a bouquet

from the lilac bush,
I almost weep
overcome by the pure

purple sweet of it all,
how perfect, how
unlikely it all is—

from the star exploding
to the first simple creature
pulling itself out of the sea

to the seed being planted
before my parents met
to the woman who is me

finding her way
to the shoulder of highway 145
where the sun has just set

and the bushes are heavy
with their honest perfume
and the air is still warm

and the stars are just
beginning to show
their old light.

Beyond the Flesh

The pears refused to be tedious.
      Thirty-eight pounds of tree-ripened fruit,
            clear juice runnelling through long, sticky fingers,
      and O such a blaze of rose blush on the yellowing skin.
One after another, I spoke to the pears
      as I quartered them, seeded them,
            and carved out their stems. "You are beautiful,"
      I said to each one. And the pears were long walks
on April afternoons. They were full moon fleshed
      and coyote song. They were slender canoes,
            a mythology of want. Candle wicks,
      innumerable coal trains, and summer coming to an end.
They were pears. And the whole house
      simmered with the white scent of Bartlett,
            not a rehearsal but the real perfume of it,
      anointing the rooms with autumnal grace.
How every breath is now laced with their loveliness.
      O summer gone. O sweetness in its place.

Still Life at Dusk

It happens surprisingly fast,
the way your shadow leaves you.

All day you've been linked by
the light, but now that darkness

gathers the world in a great black tide,
your shadow joins

the sea of all other shadows.
If you stand here long enough,

you, too, will forget your lines
and merge with the tall grass and

old trees, with the crows and the
flooding river — all these pieces

of the world that daylight has broken
into objects of singular loneliness.

It happens surprisingly fast, the drawing in
of your shadow, and standing

in the field, you become the field,
and standing in the night, you

are gathered by night. Invisible
birds sing to the memory of light

but then even those separate songs fade,
tiny drops of ink in an infinite spilling.

Climbing Impson Road at Twilight

The day is not finished, not quite —
still walking the old mining road toward tonight —

when a boy in the forest inhales juniper,
grabs his mother's hand and dances her

close to the boughs — how she beams and
breaks with his joy. How lightly she holds

his gloved hand. She inhales, blue pungency,
constellations of berries, swathes of feathery evergreen.

And inside her, the rupture, the rapture, the place
where she held him so long, so short.

Some part of her wants to fold him so small
she could slip him back into her core — that close!

And another part leans toward his brightening voice.
Her flesh, but not hers. His wonder,

her wonder, they twine in the dim. She is missing,
what? Nothing. Still the smooth stone of loss.

There is more. She is rift. She stows berries and boughs
in the deepening hole where he was.

Prayer

How's the dissolution going?
— Joi Sharp

Flatten me.
Shuck me.
Dissolve
and melt me.
Disperse me
into the air.

Scatter me.
Shatter me.
Fling and
unmatter me.
Shred, slough,
shear, split, tear.

Loose me.
Reduce me.
Erase and
untether the
small self
who compares.

Help me
abandon
any hope
I'll ever
arrive
somewhere.

Four Questions And

are you sharing it
with me, this
loneliness?

*

how do they do it,
those birds, keeping a course
through the gale
when even in this still, still room
I can hardly take one step

*

alone is more
alone than
I thought

*

as I fall
I feel how this, too,
is dancing

*

that small voice,
quiet as petals, says
why not be the one
who tears down any wall
that stands between two hearts

*

falling, falling,
I don't know when I stopped
wanting to be caught

*

new snow in the field
the only tracks there
one woman dancing

*

they sure do mess up
the sheets — excitement
and grief

*

who is the one
that falls and who is the one
who notices her falling

*

midnight.
the power out, I make
of myself a light

And For Today, That's Enough

It is hard
to unfold, day
after day,
to unfold
and open
and bloom.
Even the roses
last only a season.
See how the lilies
drop one by one
their petals
until the table
is a paean
to opening.
Save for the naked
pistil, there
is nothing
left to release.

We are not
like flowers.
There is
no rest.
It is always
the season
for opening.
And if there
are no petals
around the heart
left to unfold,
then unclose the hands.
And if the fists
are too tightly clasped,
unclose the eyes.

And if
the eyelids
are leaden,
averse,
then breathe
and follow how
inside,
the lungs
open and
open again.

The World as It Is

They are ladders,
        I tell myself, the snowflakes,
               and I could climb them

until the small white yard
        disappears in the white, white land.
               No, I tell myself,

they are kisses,
        millions and millions
               of small cold kisses.

No. They are voiceless bells
        reminding us to come to pray.
               Or lightness manifest. Or curtains

to hide our loss. Or perhaps,
        I consider, they are
               nothing more than snow,

just as a day is just a day,
        and a woman is just a woman,
               though sometimes she looks outside

of herself for a sign, looks for meaning
        in the spaces between the flakes,
               as if a drift or gust or squall might swing wide

a gate in her thoughts, but it all slips away.
        One thing for certain, I am one
               of many. One thing for certain.

I am not lost. I am here
        leaning into the windswept snowflakes, falling,
               and the field I'm in is a field, open and white.

Whole Rooms of
I Don't Know

꒷

An Afternoon with Basho

Basho sits beside the hut.

He notices the pond, the frog, the sound
made by the frog.

He does not write about it yet. He watches
for a long time. A cherry blossom falls.

He listens to the sound the water makes
without the frog.

Again. The frog. Again. Plop.

He sees himself a man wrapped around
a silence.

Perhaps you have heard it, too, the sound
the water makes before it speaks.

Perhaps you, too, have felt it,
the loneliness, the light.

And Still Some Part of Me Reaches
for a Legend, a Ruler, a Fact

*You can't solve being human. We will have this affliction till the day
we die.*
— Jeannie Zandi

I tried to know it, catch it, show it,
to splay its wings and pin them —
to chart it, graph it, plot it, map it,
quantify and reckon,

I tried to stuff it, box it, pack it,
leash it to a pole,
I wanted answers, wanted keys,
I wanted oracles,

and in came tamarisk, rodents, dust,
whole rooms of *I don't know*,
a screaming child, my milk dried up,
my fear devoured me whole.

Splintered, rumpled, rankled, crumpled,
my all collapsed, unchorused.
Undone, released, exposed, unsolved,
my shoulds all mastered, porous.

Before We Can Unlearn

So far it's the physical world that we speak of:
  the red Frisbee, the sweet blackberry, the small pink ball.
   She points to a tree. *This*, she says. *Tree*, I say. *Well,*

lilac bush. Already the world slips from its chain of phonemes.
  I want to speak with her about this filtered honey light
   of a late April afternoon, and I do, but she brings me

a rock and says, *This*. And I say, *Rock. Gray rock.*
  And even more, I want to speak of what comes next,
   of the longing that this light begets — how it rouses in me

a deep wish to lose the physical world and be current,
  be wave, be invisible flourish, to be warmth that drives flowers
   to bloom. I want to tell her how sometimes the body

interferes, so material, so fleshsome, so brute in its hungers.
  How beyond the red Frisbee there's a pulse, a rhythm,
   a tide no words can touch, that pulls us and connects

us to this all that is: one cosmos, one bloodstream, one river,
  one art. How sometimes we get it — whatever it is — and all
   that is concrete dissolves in the breath. How we're twined

to this moment, and the next, and the next. *Nest*, I say,
  as she brings me the wreath of grass. *Bird*, I say,
   as the small body wings past. She smiles and tries to fly —

half jump, half fall, all innocence. *Yes*, I say. *That's what
  love is like.* Oh golden light. Oh luminous task of losing
   whatever we think we know: Tree. Rock. Nest.

Ungraphable

How many times I've wished to carve our names
in the gray cottonwood trees across the ditch.
As if the writing of things makes them more real.
As if through etching and whittling bark, a love might
gain more permanence, or grow, perhaps, as cottonwoods do,
rapid and full of vigor. Last year, one of the largest trees lost half
    its wood,
split deep down the core and crashed to our roof. The remaining
half, a gaping carcass, still pushes out leaves, but stands deformed.

Let us write our names in water, then, for the simple pleasure
writing brings. Let us write them in star patterns, snowdrifts, mud.
Let us tap out our names in the Morse code of blood that thrums
through tender wrists, through open hands that reach
for another's grasp. And let's lose our names and see
what else might catch. Something permanent. Like love, perhaps.

Attempt

The weight of love,
it is sometimes,
to the ounce,

the weight of a man
as he rests
his body on yours.

Though if there is sorrow
or sickness in his thoughts,
the gravity can flatten you.

And sometimes it's
heavier than that, the weight,
as if he first hems his pants

with lead and then
finds his way to your arms.
And sometimes it's heavier

even than that, as if
the very air in his lungs
has millions of pockets,

all of them filled
with dull
gray stones.

And sometimes
the weight of love
is no weight at all,

is less than a blade
of orchard grass,
less than a note

hummed in quiet rooms,
less than a memory,
less than the scent

of lilac or rose,
more like the light
that lands on the hand

and invites it to open,
to hold what never
can be held.

Although It's Messy

Doubt all else. But praise.
    — John Ciardi, "White Heron"

The goldstrike apricots lay strewn on the ground,
and the warm morning wraps its many arms
around their reddening, ample orbs, translating them into

a softer, sweeter, riper meat—the kind that needs no teeth to eat it.
More juice than flesh. Their blush is an augur of happiness
that surely could stand beside the parasols and golden fish

in the Buddhist's list of eight auspicious symbols.
In my own list of promising signs, I add
the open hand. The lace of dried rice grass in the desert field.

Hummingbirds with emerald backs. The first star of night.
And the next. And the next. Heart-shaped rocks. Oval rocks.
Rocks that defy any nameable shape. Arrows. Anything orange.

Wings. And the moon in every stage. I haven't mentioned
rose petals. Unfinished circles. The lonesome scent of sage.
A winding path. The sky in blue. Or gray.

The smile in the voice when a loved one says your name.
I could not limit myself to eight auspicious signs.
Every hour the list gushes longer, more messy,

like apricot juice trickling down the chin, the neck,
the hand, the elbow, the wrist. So uncontainable in its sweetness.
So ready to escape its own skin.

And so it is with this long list of symbols
as it scribbles across the day's limbs.
So much to lead us back to our own happiness,

or as Saint Francis said, "What we are looking for
is what is looking." Deep pleasure, oh,
in the finding of auspicious things to name.

And in the perpetual looking.
In the reassuring looking.
In the looking and looking again.

So I Keep On Reckoning

Let's say that in this equation, x equals listening.
    And y equals the velvet of your hand
        behind my inner knee. And z equals

a widening gap in the clouds where the blue leaks through.
    And then p is the tongue. And q is a road of 379 miles,
        and r is the rate of what a song does in an empty room.

I don't know. What I'm saying is that I've been trying
    to solve the problem, but the variables
        keep changing. And where does dirt come into this?

Where the Brazil nut, the pelican with wings dredged in oil,
    the wildfire devouring McKenzie Springs?
        My paper is covered in pink eraser rubbings —

breathe, I think. Go slow. I try to remember the rules.
    But already x equals independence.
        And y equals flaxen light. And z equals

the river, swollen. And u
    is my hands in your hair. And f equals
        a dial tone. M equals fear. And j equals

the way I sometimes imagine an answer might
    appear if I try hard enough. And o is the sound of ripening peaches.
        No, o is the spider web in the pane.

No, o is oh, god, I don't know. And k is the velocity
    of a falcon when it falls, falls, falls
        and then surges up just before hitting earth.

And b is the room still doused in night
    before we slowly open the blinds
        to reveal twice as much sky

as the equation called for, and so many ravens.
    Nothing is ever equal. And already
        the formula is not the same as it was

one yes ago, one love ago, one here ago,
    one x ago when x equaled morning
        and y was a siren and z was slowly dissolving into white.

Just Because You Could Admit Something Once

It was easier, of course
        to say to the self, *no, I didn't say it,*
                than to walk on this evening's coals.
Easier to lie, you prefer the word "hide,"
        than to call to mind an awkward and ill-timed insight,
                to wear it like a necklace that draws the eye.
Better to rot, you think, than to be eloquent.
        Rather to break than remember the words
                you once spoke in a circle ripe with consent.
And the No tightens its hands around your neck,
        and No sees the rainbow out the closed window
                and surely, firmly, shutters the glass.
It is kinder this way, you tell yourself.
        The *No* sits in the center of the room
                and laughs.

Of the Wall

Why
do I try
to bolster the bricks?
I know
they come down
sometime.
Gravity.
Don't take it
personally.

*

It's hard
to watch
the walls
fall.
All we thought
we knew.
Translation:
I love you.
Only now,
more sky.

*

This pattern
of turning away
from the world
begins as our story
then calcifies —

it's
demolition
time

*

After re-examining
the walls, there
will be no demolition.

They are, like all matter,
mostly empty.

*

From a distance
the wall appeared
insurmountable.

And all I had to do
to move the wall
was lean into it.

*

I still cannot see
the other side.
But look around!
Look inside.
How much
vaster
the world
has become.

*

I ask my teacher
about walls.

She says, Notice them.

I ask, What's on the other side?

She says, You are.

Because We Never Know

The mind asks,
*Is it a cavern
or just a crack,
this gap
between us?*

The heart says,
*Hush, dear,
now leap.*

Forecast for Mourning

for my father-in-law

I do not know how to remember him —
his bluster, thunder, warmth, his glassy sea.
He was like weather, changing all the time.

Like two words that almost, but do not rhyme,
that's how we loved. We'd try, but seldom met.
I do not know how to remember him.

I'd hide a bit each time that he'd come in,
unsure if he would snarl or want to please.
He was like weather, changing all the time.

Drought. Flood. The rain with softest hands
that turns to hail. A mist that's miles deep.
I do not know how to remember him.

White out. And the blue sky after. Wind
that breaks the limbs. And docile morning breeze.
He was like weather, changing all the time.

The memories rearrange like leaves in autumn.
What is this nagging urge to rake them neat?
I do not know how to remember him.
He was like weather, changing all the time.

All in an Effort to Not Think About

Rise,
stretch
bathe, dry,

crack, whisk,
sizzle, fry,

then drive, dash, do

cross the list
red-lined through

hike, teach,
call, reach

meet
eat

brush
rush

slide
hide

cry
lie.

Nomenclature

So long I've lived
beneath the same brown birds
and still I do not know
which song belongs to which.
So long I've walked
through this meadow
and still I refer to all
the tall green stems as grass.
So long I've sat across from you
and still I wonder
who you are.
Oh, do you hear it?
One of those birds,
how it sings
so beautifully,
even in the dark.

How We're Led, Perhaps

What primarily concerns me is the necessity for a student to learn to be
as awake as possible in each moment.
— Charlotte Joko Beck, from "Life's Not a Problem"
(Tricycle, *Summer 1998*)

Perhaps we're just not ready yet to be
awake. It's so damn sweeter, mmm, to curl
inside ourselves than trust the fickle world
with all its storms, late hail and frost. And we
are tired — the winter's tough. Our sluggish knees
would rather hug the ribcage than unfurl.
Rag-arms tuck in, and we become more swirl
of bud than lush of bloom. More root than leaf,

more earth than limb, more tired than you or I
have ever been. And so we sleep and dream
of sun and blossoming — so weary that
we miss what's happening: the warming sigh
that trebles through the field; how we too green
like spring's first grass. Between our snores, god laughs.

Though All Around Us, Entropy

It holds things in —
the bile, the bones,
the heart that floats,
the glands, the spleen.
It cages the pulse

and encases the dance
of corpuscles
and ligaments.
It holds what's left
of this woman who weeps,

and it does not scar
after runnels of tears.
It shows the years
that passed but does
not tell their secrets.

It holds the brain,
the gut, the tongue,
even the heaving
of race-run lungs,
and tries to be

a container for grief,
but it leaks, the skin,
and grief, it spills,
it rushes, stampedes,
unravels and floods.

And likewise messy
are joy and bliss,
unreeling
and keeling
escape artists.

It's just doing
the task it knows
best, the skin,
dutifully trying
to hold it all in.

Instead of Dreaming

Beauty more than bitterness makes the heart break.
— Sara Teasdale, "Vignettes Overseas"

Praise the hourglass of night
with its sand that falls, that falls
and slowly wears away the layers

we put on throughout the day.
Praise the exhaustion that comes
with the long work of peeling the fruit

and filling jars with white
moon of pear and sunshine
of peach. How they become us

as we eat. And praise the ache
that comes with love when
we find ourselves alone in the small

hours of morning, warming
the home with boiling, with steam,
the hands so full, so empty.

At the Botanic Gardens

All morning we were led
by the scent of peonies,
lilacs, roses, and some white
flower on a tall maroon stem
whose name we never found.
Grass paths. Wood chip paths.
Paths with small gray stones.
And a moongate with no door —
only an opening on both sides.
You on one side, me on the other
and both of us in the middle
of something so beautiful —
walking with no purpose,
the way that rain falls,
the way that petals fall
and scatter. I want to tell you
it will last forever. Instead,
I hold your hand and say
your name.

Lullaby

> *If I lay here, if I just lay here, will you lay with me and just forget the world.*
>
> — Snow Patrol, "Chasing Cars"

Like sipping the stars in water,
like hearing the sun in stone
all the impossibles, all the fantastic
notions are possible now,

like drinking gray sky in big gulps,
like song spiraling out of bent wheat.
There is improbable joy, my love,
in the imperfect, marred, defeated.

There are shoulds, my dear, and mustn'ts
there are cages we think are ourselves,
but night is here and soon there will be
nothing we can't have.

But it's not about the having,
not even about the dream.
It's about, well, darling, I don't know.
Let's close our eyes and see.

Not That I Would Go Back

But there was that night
      on the red sandstone beach
            when the air had begun
                  to lose its swelter

and the sun was low enough
      to cast that amber light
            in which it seems easier
                  to fall in love with the world,

with the day, and with each other,
      and we had escaped
            the dinner hour,
                  the carrots half-cooked

atop the stove and the table
      not yet set. Instead
            we walked across the field
                  and plunged into the cool water.

How I loved you that night,
      the broad thrill on your face
            as you let the current carry you.
            How I loved to be

the woman in the chill water beside you
      wanting no life but this one,
            faint scent of river breeze,
                  warm desert air, bright sound of cicada

encircling the beach, the field,
      the home with the napkins still in the drawer,
            and all around us, inside of us,
                  so much ripening.

Ashes We Are Not Yet

This Being Human

A gift for you my heart would bring – the sweet release of everything,
the breath I take before I sing...
— Jan Garrett, JD Martin and Lisa Aschmann,
"The Spaces In Between Us"

This is what
we were born for —

the almost unbearable
softness of grass,

the sweet perfume
of blue weeds in spring,

listening for voices
that cannot be heard,

and reaching for that
which can never be held.

The popping sound
of the daffodil bloom,

having our hearts
ripped open, and again.

The weeping, the salt,
the communion of blood.

The new leafing out
of the old cottonwood tree

and the long walk
to the cemetery.

Oh this beautiful ache
of the ashes

we are not yet.

Waiting the Diagnosis

I bow to the ache of it,
the deep inner eating
away at itself, I bow
to the shivers, the gooseflesh,
the waves of nausea and pain.
I bow to the unnamed,
to question, to dark.
And I bow to the fear
that crowds into the kitchen
and the I-don't-know-what
that sometimes drives out the fear.
I bow to every other human
who hurts and I bow
to the yellow flowers tonight
blooming in the muck
where the river used to be.
I bow to the ache, goddammit,
I bow to it and I bow
to the reluctance to bow to it,
bow to the longing to shove
it all away, and I bow,
hush now, just bow.

And Now It Is Morning

*And I, infinitesimal being, / drunk with the great starry /
void, / likeness, image of / mystery, / I felt myself a pure part /
of the abyss, / I wheeled with the stars, / my heart broke loose
on the wind.*
      — Pablo Neruda, "Poetry"

Oh Pablo, I've felt it, too, stardrunk
and spinning with the miracle
of it all. Tiny and infinite.

I've walked in the generous mantle of night
and lost my name, lost
my thoughts, lost my limbs,

lost everything except
my praise and gratitude.
And then, from this blissreeling

oneness, this wide open wheeling, I've walked
in the front door and vacuumed.
And cleaned scum from the tub.

And used a shrill voice with my son.
And wished for things I do not have.
It is easier, sometimes, to be dissolved

into starlight. Easier to define myself
as daughter of the universe than
as mother to a toddler and six-year-old boy.

It's easier to melt into the night
than to be a woman who wants, who fails,
who tries. But given the choice,

I would stay here on this earth
with its lures and fears, with its vices
and corpses and vacuums and naming of things.

I am practicing what it means to be a woman,
Pablo, and it helps to read your words,
to know that you, too, great lover of flesh

sometimes loosed your self on the wind.

Feeding the Hungry

In our eagerness for conceptual meanings, we ignore the actual beast.
— James Hillman, "Dream Animals"

It was no metaphor I bit into tonight
    but the real apple, sweet white flesh, crisp,
a thin red and green skinned Gala picked from the tree
    in the center of the garden surrounded by snakes,
not metaphorical snakes, but the real ones, reticulated skin,
    long forked tongues a-flicker, all glisten and slither and hiss.

And it is no metaphorical night tonight, but the real one, dim,
    with half of a milksome moon mounting the real horizon.
And the loneliness, that is real, too, though I cannot point to it,
    touch it, nor bite it. Nor can it bite me. Nor does the darkness
dislocate its jaw to swallow me whole.
    Nor does the moon illumine my mind.

But the apple does make it a sweeter solitude
    as I think of you, the real you,
and all the skins we've shed, discarded, how many times
    we've launched anew, and how I wish
your very real skin were nearer in this dim,
    your hand reaching for what's left of the core.

What Isn't Mine

No not this day with all its sudden snow
and not the sunshine sliding through the white.
Not my children, though I call them mine
and feed them, drive them where they need to go.
My car? It's in my husband's name. My home?
The bank owns part of it. The words I write?
I steal from all my heroes. My delight?
I learned it from my mother. There is no
computer, cell phone, cookbook, shirt or cat
that I can point to and say *I own that* —
for anything I think is mine can steal
away like snow in sun or autumn leaves
in trees. The less I hold the more I feel
whatever owns the trees is living me.

Going In

The way the river meets our bodies,
meet me that way. If I resist,

surround me. Rush to me.
Drench me. Insist. Touch me

everywhere and at once. Float me.
Ignore my name.

Leave me, arriving.
Bring news of the sky.

Slumber me. Wake me. The years go by.
We are both more ourselves and less.

Meet me how the river meets
our bodies, with countless tongues,

every one thirsty, every one
curious. Surprise me with your

strength, your pull. Say nothing.
Meet me. My hands are stone.

Erode me. Soften me. Release me
in you. You stretch in both directions

as far as I can see.

At Four

We bring our deaths everywhere we go.
— Susan Tweit, "Walking Nature Home"

He wanted to know
why he had to
wear his seat belt. I
wanted to tell him,

We bring our deaths
with us everywhere we
go. Instead, I said,
Because I love you

too much to argue.
He said, *I love*
you, too, mom, put
on your seat belt.

This is what I
want to remember: the
smell of the river,
the brrrr-eeeee-ahk of the

red-winged black birds
trilling through the open
window, the feeling of
the strap over my

heart, tethering me to
the slant light, the
rotting leaves at the
river bottom, my son,

and death hiding in
the car, strapped in
with us, perhaps
laughing.

I Like Its Hows

i like my body when it is with your body. it's so quite new a thing.
— e.e. cummings, "i like my body when it is with your"

I like the way he slips his willow body next to mine,
then folds his head into my neck and nuzzles deeper in.
He hums a little drowsy morning hum that bends the dim.

I like his hum. I like the way it has no words, the way
it lacks a tune, is pleasure driven. Warmish. Wordless. His.
And mmm, the width of skin across his head, a place to kiss,

and kiss, and kiss again. The thick astonishment of hair
that I will yet again breathe in, and press my cheek to where
the fontanel once was, remember how his skull pressed hard

against my core and widened me, the lavish praise of blood,
the body in its ecstasy O! thrusting new life forth.
The ohm of after pushing him. His wail. His tiny lips.

The slow pink dawn of miracle. The shocking surge of yes.
I like to feel his spine now, how it curves against my womb.
The boy so grown, so fledged at five, his body still so new.

Meanwhile, in Another Garden

tsstsstsstsstsstsstsstsstss
      and from short grass beside the wire fence
            the serpent rises, a lean silhouette,
      and frames the low orange sunset in its angle of mouth.
I hear the rattle more than see the coil,
      but coil it does and raises high its diamond head.
            I want to reach and touch it,
      become acquainted with its slither,
know the fangs, the frenzied tail.
      But something in me steps away. Then something else
          says *Step closer again,*
      and so I do, *tsstsstsstsstss.*
The baby in my arms makes not a stir
      but I am well aware of her
          and slowly turn to walk toward home
      humming her name,
one hand strokes her hair,
      one hand reaches back.

Vivian Learns Present Progressive

Mama chasing me, she says,
and she runs with her small feet

tilt-syncopated and youth drunk
and for the first time she *–ings*

in her speech, and the moment
leaps out of the present and leans

into the thought that an object
in motion remains in motion

and life scampers on past
this frame

where she and I race around
the green countertop. And the present,

once all there was, grows wings. And it's true,
I am chasing, have chased and will still

be chasing her long after her squeal
has left its sender to find the moon.

We push toward the future so soon and then
spend a whole lifetime trying to unlearn

the present progressive, to wholly embrace
what is now. I chase. I crave. I learn. We reach,

and I would make the seconds hover
if I could, and still all my longing and slow

the light as it leaves. But morning
slips its scaffolding and she's lying in bed

tonight cooing the alphabet in gibberish, a verb
who is falling but has not yet quite fallen asleep.

While from the Kitchen Wafts the Scent
of Something Burning on the Stove

Flipping through the magazine
I find an ad for my life. They are selling it
at a discount — 20 percent off if you call
this month. The children are smiling.

Their clothes are clean, their hair
brushed, and in the picture they
are picking up their yard toys, laughing.
My husband, very handsome, smiles at me adoringly,

and I smile back. My teeth are perfect,
though a tad yellow, my smile real.
My Volvo, sea foam with tan seats,
must have just been through the car wash,

and it shines in the golden light beside the garden,
which is weeded and hoed. The lettuce,
already up, is thinned, and at least
from this distance there are no aphids

in the leaves. In the upper left,
the solar eclipse has just begun, and
there is a sense that the birdsong
in the picture has just quieted

so that one might better hear
the hushed rush of the river, not pictured.
In the lower right corner
an asterisk hidden in the perfect yellow tulips

snuggles up against
some very fine print that mentions
how the picture is merely a suggestion.
I know that the next four pages

will be black and white text, 8 point,
with testimonies from my friends,
my parents, my therapists. They will
divulge all the secrets I tried for years

to hide under my skin. Six columns
of side effects: A predilection toward
weeping in public. Inability to remember
important dates. Addictions to Diet Pepsi, and

listening to a cappella versions of Lady Gaga.
Aversion to going to sleep. Perfectionism. Erroneous
belief in an ability to mind read. Decades
of low self esteem. There is more. I laugh

at the disclaimer about lack of boundaries
and refusal to see it as a problem. Oh please.
I flip the page to read an article on the Science of Nothing,
but halfway through the first paragraph

I flip back to the ad, take a slug of Diet Pepsi,
and shout at the kids to stop bickering
so I can make a phone call.
I'm ready to offer full price.

Nine Dismantlings

my hammer, my nails
what good are they now
the whole roof collapsed

*

doe in the meadow
my thoughts in the meadow
one of these is quiet

*

so much to learn
about
not knowing

*

not by the shoulders
but by the soul
life shakes me

*

hands bloody
tearing down a wall
that isn't even there

*

doe in the meadow
my thoughts in the meadow
one of these is quiet

*

at the same time
the tree grows
toward darkness, toward light

*

so open my hands
not holding
my hammer, my nails

*

surrounded by rubble
still I beg *Love, keep having*
your way with me

A Long Farewell

The world breaks everyone and afterward many are strong in the broken places. But those that will not break it kills. It kills the very good and the very gentle and the very brave impartially. If you are none of these you can be sure it will kill you too but there will be no special hurry.
— Ernest Hemingway, A Farewell to Arms

Dear World,

Thank you for breaking me.

The rabbit brush are in full bloom.
Yellow in the field. Yesterday
I mowed the edges of the drive
and as a matter of course
I mowed whatever rabbit brush
was in my path. The air
smelled so good then,
a clean, sharp scent,
almost like sage,
only quieter.

I have not been very good.
I have not been very gentle.
I have not been very brave.
But I have been sincere.
And I have loved.

There was a time when
I wanted to weed all the rabbit brush
from the field. I wanted only field grass.
I would wait for it to rain for days,
then pull up as much rabbit brush as I could.

World, I have not been very good.
And you have broken me so perfectly —
always leading me to just the right place
for falling apart. World, how do you do that?

The rabbit brush always comes back
and eventually I learned to leave them
wherever they leap up. And eventually I learned
to find them beautiful.

I have not been very gentle, world.
I have taken what I wanted, sometimes mercilessly.
And you take every opportunity to kill me,
sometimes with fear, sometimes
with beauty, great or small.

Yellow. Yellow. Yellow.
Thousands of yellow hands
all waving each time I arrive.

World, I have not been very brave.
I am not like Hemingway. When the war comes
I try to hide. And still you come to kill me
like a warrior, like a soldier,
only much, much slower.

The rabbit brush does not mind drought.
It thrives in cracked, parched soil.
The rabbit brush does not mind the rain.
It thrives. It thrives.

I can't say I like being broken, world.
I can't say I like being killed.
But you do it so well and I do admire
your insuperable skill. Keep killing me,
world, keep breaking me. Keep finding
my flaws. Press until I crack.
I am broken, dying, thriving. I am waving
at you waving back.

Winter Song

The seasons always change. And life will find a way.
— Sara Bareilles, "Winter Song"

Cracked, the sidewalk,
and snapped, the branches,
and bent the dead weeds

with their shriveled leaves
weary like prayer flags spent.
Even the rocks are chipped

and the smell of decay
weaves into the breeze.
There is nothing on this

late autumn walk
that seems whole, which is to say
everything is broken together —

me, the weeds, the sad concrete.
Even so, this odd heart,
ripening out of season,

chooses to fall deeper in love
with the world, though the forecast
is for cold and getting colder.

End Notes

Epistemology
This poem grew in part out of a line from Lew Welch, "I saw my-self a ring of bone," a line which often plays in my head, and then it found an Emily Dickinson-ish form. It makes me laugh to think of this particular pairing of poets sorta snuggling on the same page.

The Sail Opens
In Daniel Ladinsky's *Love Poems from God: Twelve Sacred Voices from the East and West* (Penguin, 2002), he begins one of his renderings of Rumi this way, "On a day when the wind is perfect, the sail just needs to open and the world is full of beauty, today is such a day."

Still Life at Dusk
This poem reminds me of a song performed by Libana, with the lyrics attributed to Rainer Maria Rilke, which says, "Night goes back to where it was. Everyone returns home sometime. Night when you get there, tell them how I love you." It was not until one night in the hills above my home in Placerville that I began to un-derstand what he meant. While standing still during a hike, when I noticed how the setting sun created a wave of darkness that sub-sumed my own shadow. It was so fun to watch, I kept racing ahead of it to watch it happen again and again and again until finally the night took all.

Climbing Impson Road at Twilight
This poem was inspired by my son, Finn. When he was four, we were on the walk described in this poem and he said, *It's so beautiful, I can barely concentrate on walking. I only want to smell juniper berries.*

Four Questions And
The last haiku in this sequence refers to the reported last words of the Buddha, Make of yourself a light.

Of the Wall
This poem was created as part of a poetry dialogue with poet Barry Spacks. It is written in a conversational form that he created, in

which two poets take turns sending each other 84-character poems on a chosen theme. The number 84 is symbolic of the Buddha's 84,000 teachings. "Of the Wall" contains only poems that I wrote, and is excerpted from a much longer sequence that contains poems by both of us.

All in an Effort to Not Think About

This poem is one of many I wrote in response to the death of poet Karen Chamberlain, who greatly influenced the way I think about poetry and a poetry community. Her book, *Ephedra* (People's Press, 2012), published posthumously, is one of the books I never bother to put on the shelf, knowing it will be out again soon.

This Being Human

The epigraph for this poem comes from such a lovely, haunting song. One day, well, more than one, I couldn't get this song out of my head and the poem grew in part from that soundtrack. The musicians, Jan Garrett and JD Martin, are friends of mine and have so many songs that have moved with me through life's doors. To hear more, visit them at garrett-martin.com.

What Isn't Mine

This poem was inspired by a poem by Veronica Patterson by the same title, found in her stunning book *Thresh & Hold* (Big Pencil Press, 2009). After reading her poem, I became fascinated with this kind of a list and have written several variations. And so when I gave some of my poetry students the assignment to write a sonnet in ten minutes (!), I wrote along with them and this list was the first theme that popped into my head. Though I love tinkering with poems long after they've been written, this one I kept intact in its original ten-minute version, perhaps an homage to even this poem not being mine, not even its title.

At Four

After reading *Walking Nature Home: A Life's Journey* (University of Texas, 2009), by my friend Susan Tweit, I had a new relationship with life, which is also to say a new relationship with death. The book is a remarkable accounting of healing our relationships with each other, our selves and our planet.

I Like Its Hows

The title for this poem, and even some of the phrasing, comes from the e.e. cummings poem "i like my body when it is with your." The poem was inspired in part by Jack Mueller, one of my poetic heroes, who challenged me one night to write sensually about motherhood. He was lamenting how that sensuality can be taboo, too many people willing to misinterpret the intimacy.

Turkey Buzzard Press Catalog

Michael Adams
Broken Hand Peak, a poem, 9 pages, 2008
      ISBN 0-945884-24-9; distributed free at poetry readings
If You Can Still Dance With It, poetry, 36 pages, 2012
      ISBN 0-945884-38-9; $12.00

Kathryn T.S. Bass
The Mysteries, poetry, 58 pages, 2011
      ISBN 0-945884-36-2; $16.00

Maria Berardi
Cassandra Gifts, poetry, 48 pages, 2012
      ISBN 0-945884-39-7; $12.00

Janet Glovinsky
Bird in Hand, poetry and art, 72 pages, 2010
      (oversized, 20 full-color plates, four black and white)*
      ISBN 978-0-945884-32-3; $25.00

Hildegard Guttendorfer
one feather more, poetry, 52 pages, 2009
      ISBN 978-0-945884-30-9; $10.00

John Macker
Underground Sky, poetry, 89 pages, 2010
      ISBN 978-0-945884-33-0; $15.00
Woman of the Disturbed Earth, poetry, 39 pages, 2007
      ISBN 0-945884-21-4; $10.00

Murray Moulding
Moon Over Easy, poetry, 36 pages, 2009
      ISBN 978-0-945884-31-6; $10.00

John Nizalowski
The Last Matinée, poetry, 75 pages, 2011
      ISBN 0-945884-35-4; $12.00

David Patton
The Trinity, poetry and art, 40 pages, 2008
      ISBN 0-945884-26-5; $10.00

Turkey Buzzard Press Catalog

Jerry Smaldone
All Flesh Shall See It Together, poetry, 44 pages, 2009
ISBN 0-945884-28-1; $10.00

Padma Jared Thornlyre
Eating Totem: The Mossbeard Poems, 48 pages, 2008
ISBN 0-945884-23-0; $10.00
Mavka: a poem in 50 parts, 22 pages, 2011 (oversized)*
ISBN 0-945884-37-0; $20.00

Rosemerry Wahtola Trommer
Holding Three Things at Once, poetry, 61 pages, 2008
ISBN 0-945884-27-3; $15.00
The Less I Hold, poetry, 71 pages, 2012
ISBN 0-945884-41-9; $15.00

Eric Walter
Moves Between Worlds, poetry, 62 pages, 2012
ISBN 0-945884-40-0; $12.00

Donna Wise
River Beneath the River, poetry, 41 pages, 2007
ISBN 0-945884-20-6; $10.00

Phil Woods
Lucid Dreaming, poetry, 53 pages, 2010
ISBN 0-945884-34-6; $12.00
Original Mind, poetry, 34 pages, 2008
ISBN 0-945884-25-7; $10.00

Phil Woods, Michael Adams and James Taylor III
Whistleblowers: The Free Radical Railroad
poetry anthology, 69 pages, 2009
ISBN 0-945884-29-X; $12.00

Please add $2.00 shipping/handling for one to three titles and $4.00 for four titles or more. Make checks or money orders payable to:

Turkey Buzzard Press
P.O. Box 354
Kittredge, CO 80457

* Please add an additional $2.00 per copy for oversized titles.